X-TREME FACTS: NATURAL DISASTERS

HURRICANES

by Marcia Abramson

Minneapolis, Minnesota

Credits:
Title Page, 4 top, 11 top, 11 bottom, 17 bottom, 28 bottom left, NASA/Public Domain; 4 bottom, oneinchpunch/Shutterstock; 5 top, FotoKina/Shutterstock; 5 top right, chaiyapruek youprasert/Shutterstock; 5 middle, Drew McArthur/Shutterstock; 5 middle right, Regine Poirier/Shutterstock.com; 5 bottom, Library of Congress/Public Domain; 6 top, Viacheslav Lopatin/Shutterstock; 6 bottom, GOLFX/Shutterstock; 7 top left, Daderot/Creative Commons; 7 top. Henry Donati/Department for International Development/Creative Commons; 7 top right, Fab_1/Shutterstock; 7 middle, Glynnis Jones/Shutterstock.com; 7 bottom, elwynn/Shutterstock; 8, Benny Marty/Shutterstock; 8 left, Jeka/Shutterstock; 8 right, Vector Shutterstock/Shutterstock; 9 top, vivanvu/Shutterstock; 9 top left, Milkovasa/Shutterstock; 9, Tongsai/Shutterstock; 9 bottom right, New Africa/Shutterstock; 10 top, 11 middle, 15 bottom, 25 top, 25 middle, 25 bottom right, NOAA/Public Domain;10 bottom, Kelvinsong/Creative Commons; 11 top right, Prostock-studio/Shutterstock; 12 145Patma/Shutterstock; 12 left, Dustie/Shutterstock.com;12 right, Mama Belle and the kids/Shutterstock; 13 top, Simeonn/Shutterstock; 13 middle, Harvepino/Shutterstock; 13 bottom, IrinaK/Shutterstock; 14 ccpixx photography/Shutterstock.com; 15 top, 18 bottom, 20 top, 20 middle, Jocelyn Augusitno/FEMA/Public Domain; 15 top right, Gelpi/Shutterstock; 16 top, mkfilm/Shutterstock; 16 top middle, Evtushkova Olga/Shutterstock; 16 middle, Lawrence Ruiz/Creative Commons; 16 bottom, 19 bottom left, 22 right, 27 top left, LightField Studios/Shutterstock; 17 top, jokerpro/Shutterstock; 17 top left, Rommel Canlas/Shutterstock; 17 top middle, Burry van den Brink/Shutterstock; 17 top right, Phil Stev/Shutterstock; 17 bottom left, CGN089/Shutterstock; 18 top, FotoKina/Shutterstock; 18 top right, Cast Of Thousands/Shutterstock; 19 top, MDay Photography/Shutterstock; 19 middle, Terry Kelly/Shutterstock.com; 19 bottom, CBP Photography/Public Domain; 19 bottom right, Happy Together/Shutterstock; 20 bottom, Roosevelt Skerrit/Creative Commons; 21 top, Jill Carlson/Creative Commons; 21 top middle, Tatyana Vyc/Shutterstock; 21 bottom, Jon Rehg/Shutterstock.com; 21 bottom left, Steve Byland/Shutterstock; 21 bottom right, warat42/Shutterstock; 22 Drepicter/Shutterstock; 22 left, Olena Yakobchuk/Shutterstock; 23 top, VILTVART/Shutterstock.com; 23 top right, Michael C. Gray/Shutterstock; 23, Holly Mazour/Shutterstock; 23 bottom middle, Jat306/Shutterstock; 24 Ste Everington/Shutterstock; 24 left, fizkes/Shutterstock; 24 right, John Gomez/Shutterstock; 25 middle right, Tinseltown/Shutterstock.com; 26 V.Borisov/Shutterstock; 26 bottom left, PRESSLAB/Shutterstock; 26 bottom right, Edgar G Biehle/Shutterstock; 27 Terry Kelly/Shutterstock.com; 27 top right, Sonpichit Salangsing/Shutterstock; 27, Team New Orleans, US Army Corps of Engineers/Public Domain; 27 bottom right, P. Mullins/Shutterstock; 28 top left, Repina Valeriya/Shutterstock; 28-29, Austen Photography

Bearport Publishing Company Product Development Team
President: Jen Jenson; Director of Product Development: Spencer Brinker; Managing Editor: Allison Juda; Associate Editor: Naomi Reich; Associate Editor: Tiana Tran; Senior Designer: Colin O'Dea; Associate Designer: Elena Klinkner; Associate Designer: Kayla Eggert; Product Development Specialist: Anita Stasson

Produced for Bearport Publishing by BlueAppleWorks Inc.
Managing Editor for BlueAppleWorks: Melissa McClellan
Art Director: T.J. Choleva
Photo Research: Jane Reid

Library of Congress Cataloging-in-Publication Data is available at www.loc.gov or upon request from the publisher.

ISBN: 979-8-88509-981-3 (hardcover)
ISBN: 979-8-88822-161-7 (paperback)
ISBN: 979-8-88822-301-7 (ebook)

Copyright © 2024 Bearport Publishing Company. All rights reserved. No part of this publication may be reproduced in whole or in part, stored in any retrieval system, or transmitted in any form or by any means, electronic, mechanical, photocopying, recording, or otherwise, without written permission from the publisher.

For more information, write to Bearport Publishing, 5357 Penn Avenue South, Minneapolis, MN 55419.

Contents

Inside the Storm	4
Weather of Mass Destruction	6
Where Do They Come From?	8
Parts of the Storm	10
End of the Fury	12
Extreme Surges	14
This Will Blow You Away!	16
Categorized	18
Deadly Lessons	20
Bigger and Badder	22
Hunting for Clues	24
Fighting Hurricanes	26
Your Own Spin	28
Glossary	30
Read More	31
Learn More Online	31
Index	32
About the Author	32

Inside the Storm

Sheets of rain slash down from a dark sky. Fierce winds send heavy objects flying through the air. The noise is deafening as the storm rages. Then, a sudden quiet settles in as the **eye** passes over. But the calm won't last for long as one of the strongest kinds of storms on Earth barrels forward. Take cover—it's a hurricane!

China, the Philippines, and Japan have gotten the most hurricanes in the past 50 years.

NO FAIR! WE NEVER GET ANY HURRICANES HERE!

AREN'T OUR SANDSTORMS ENOUGH FOR YOU?

Want to avoid hurricanes? Visit Qatar. This country in the Middle East is the place least likely to be hit by a hurricane.

Weather of Mass Destruction

Hurricanes are strong storms that form over warm ocean water. As they rush toward shore, hurricanes bring dangerous weather that leaves massive amounts of destruction in its wake. The rotating weather systems can include heavy rain, strong winds, and even tornadoes. Hurricanes damage and destroy buildings, roads, and bridges.

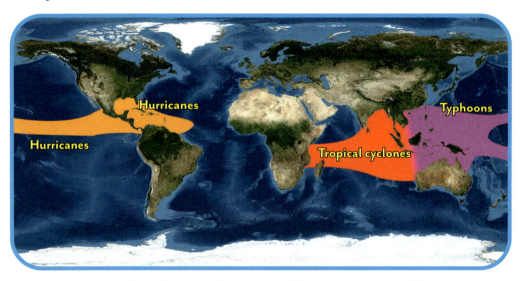

Hurricanes, tropical cyclones, and typhoons are different names for the same kind of storm. The name depends on where the storm forms.

JUST LIKE MY COUSIN ALICE. SHE'S ALWAYS LATE, TOO!

The Atlantic hurricane season usually lasts from June to November. But it seems no one told Hurricane Alice that! Alice arrived in December 1954—the latest ever.

Hurakan was a Mayan god of storms.

THAT WAS ONE NASTY HURACÁN!

WE CALL IT A TYPHOON! BUT IT GETS JUST AS NASTY.

Spanish people in the Caribbean called this kind of harsh storm *huracán* after the name used by the people from the area. This soon became the word *hurricane* in English.

The word *typhoon* has a more mysterious origin. It may have come from ancient Greece, Arabia, or China—or all of them.

As they sweep through a city, hurricanes can knock out power and water supplies. They can also destroy animal habitats on land and in the ocean.

7

Where Do They Come From?

Any hot, sunny day in the tropics can disguise brewing trouble. A hurricane begins when an area of low pressure, called a tropical wave or depression, moves in. Warm ocean air swirls up into the low pressure system where it cools and **condenses** to form clouds. The cycle repeats over and over, and all that moving air generates wind. Earth's rotation gives the clouds and wind an extra push to spin, and a hurricane is born!

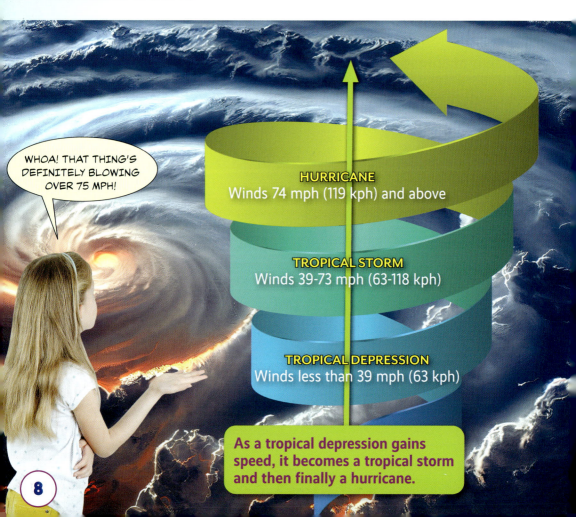

WHOA! THAT THING'S DEFINITELY BLOWING OVER 75 MPH!

HURRICANE
Winds 74 mph (119 kph) and above

TROPICAL STORM
Winds 39-73 mph (63-118 kph)

TROPICAL DEPRESSION
Winds less than 39 mph (63 kph)

As a tropical depression gains speed, it becomes a tropical storm and then finally a hurricane.

Warm air holds lots of moisture, which is just what hurricanes need. As they suck it up, hurricanes get bigger and stronger.

Hurricanes don't form until the water temperature hits 80 degrees Fahrenheit (27 degrees Celsius).

Hurricanes spin counterclockwise north of the equator and clockwise south of it.

Parts of the Storm

These powerful weather systems have three main parts. A hurricane twists around a calm center called the eye. The weather in the eye is often mostly cloud-free with a light breeze. But surrounding the eerie quiet of the eye, you'll find the **eyewall**. Here, the storm's tallest clouds and strongest winds make up the most dangerous part of the storm. Just beyond that are **rainbands** of intense thunderstorms, strong winds, and sometimes even tornadoes.

Hurricane Ivan was a tornado-making machine. It **spawned** a record 177 tornadoes over the course of just a few days in 2004.

Hurricane structure

End of the Fury

Eventually, hurricanes fizzle into a drizzle. Some turn inland and, after making **landfall**, run out of energy without the warm ocean air to suck up. Others head out into colder waters and slow down for the same reason. Strong winds coming from the opposite direction can also bring about the end. This weather pattern, known as **wind shear**, disrupts a hurricane's rotation. As the storm breaks apart, its clouds and rain scatter far and wide, and the sun peeks out again.

A hurricane can reform if it crosses warm seas again after it makes landfall.

Running into a bigger hurricane can weaken a smaller one. This happened to Hurricane Julia when it met with Hurricane Igor in 2010.

When two big hurricanes get close, they may join up!

A hurricane can last an entire month if it doesn't make landfall or experience wind shear. In 1994, one giant storm hung over the Pacific Ocean for a record 31 days.

Even after they break up, hurricanes can still cause damage. The resulting rainstorms can send serious flooding rains inland.

Extreme Surges

One of the biggest hurricane-related dangers can come after the storm. Strong hurricane winds push ocean water toward the shore. This is called a storm surge. Often, there is enough water to flow over protective **levees** and **seawalls**. This dangerous flooding may causes many deaths. What makes it even more deadly is the timing. A storm surge typically hits shortly after a hurricane passes. People may think they are finally safe, but then water quickly rushes in around them.

Sea, Lake, and Overland Surges from Hurricanes (SLOSH) is a computer model that forecasters use to try and predict storm surges.

THIS SURGE WAS PREDICTED BY SLOSH.

WHAT A PERFECT NAME FOR IT!

SLOSH

SPLOOSH

SPLASH

SLOSH

Most surges are over quickly. The water often flows back to the ocean after only a few hours.

I'M SO HAPPY THE STORM TIDE IS GONE!

YEAH, IT DOESN'T LOOK VERY TIDY OUT THERE, DOES IT?

A storm surge during **high tide** is called a storm tide. Storm tides have more water and are even more destructive.

The unofficial world record for highest storm surge was for one that hit Australia in 1899. It is thought to have been more than 40 feet (12 m) high.

In 2005, nearly 80 percent of New Orleans, Louisiana, was submerged by a storm surge from Hurricane Katrina. Some of the water was high enough to completely cover homes.

This Will Blow You Away!

Between torrential rains, winds, tornadoes, and storm surges, it's no wonder these extreme storms set some serious weather records. Whether making landfall as hurricanes, cyclones, or typhoons, the storms have brought chaos and devastation in many forms. From the most rainfall to the strongest winds, which of these big weathermakers top the extreme charts?

Cyclone Denise dropped nearly 72 inches (2 m) of rain in just 24 hours. That's a world record.

BIG DEAL. I CAN THROW THIS BALL FURTHER!

Typhoon Haiyan tossed a 177-ton (160-t) boulder 150 ft (45 m). That's another record.

Categorized

How do we measure how strong these storms are as they come slamming onto land? In the United States, each hurricane gets a rating from category 1 to 5 on the **Saffir-Simpson Wind Scale**. The lowest category includes winds whipping at only 74-95 miles per hour (119-153 kph). The numbers get higher as a storm grows and gains strength. On the extreme end of the scale, a category 5 storm has windspeeds over 157 miles per hour (252 kph)!

Other world regions have their own name and numbering systems for hurricanes.

NO MATTER WHAT CATEGORY, TREES ARE ALWAYS IN TROUBLE.

During category 1 storms, weak trees might be torn up and loose shingles can go flying.

Category 2 storms are a bit more powerful. **They can have winds up to 110 miles per hour (180 kph).**

Category 2 storms may cause power outages that can last for weeks.

18

With category 3 storms, winds can speed up to 129 miles per hour (208 kph) and storm surges may reach 12 ft (3.7 m). Buildings can be seriously damaged.

Category 4 storms may leave areas unlivable for months. They have winds up to 156 miles per hour (251 kph).

Category 5 storms are the strongest. Winds whip above 157 miles per hour (252 kph) and storm surges are likely to be over 18 ft (5.5 m) high.

WHAT HAPPENED HERE?

HURRICANE DORIAN HAPPENED. CATEGORY 5!

19

Deadly Lessons

Some of the most devastating hurricanes of all time took place during the twenty-first century. The storm season of 2005 brought many hard lessons with four killer storms in a row. The destruction from Emily and Katrina was followed by devastating hurricanes Rita and Wilma. Cleaning up and providing aid after such extreme weather is a challenge. Relief efforts may take time and leave people without food, water, and electricity.

After Hurricane Katrina, thousands of people had to be rescued from their rooftops. Many were brought to safety by boat.

In 2017, it took about 11 months to get the power back in Puerto Rico after Hurricane Maria.

The names of deadly storms like Katrina and Maria are retired. They are never used again.

Bigger and Badder

Unfortunately, devastating storms might be getting worse. As **climate change** heats the ocean, there's more warm air to fuel hurricanes, making them bigger and stronger. This warmer air also impacts wind patterns, creating better conditions for hurricanes. In recent years, hurricanes Michael, Harvey, Irma, Maria, Florence, and Patricia all surprised scientists by how quickly they grew. Without action against climate change, these powerful storms will likely only get worse.

More categories may be added to the Saffir-Simpson Scale because hurricanes are getting so strong.

Warmer water lets hurricanes form further north and head for Europe. They've even reached the Swiss Alps.

One way to combat rising temperatures is to rely more on clean energy, such as that from solar and wind power.

NOW, THAT'S ONE SOLAR POWERHOUSE!

Hurricanes themselves might someday provide clean energy! Japanese engineers are working to create a device that can harness their power.

HOW DO WE CATCH ALL THAT ENERGY?

The wind from just two hurricanes can produce as much energy as all of the world's power plants put together.

DO YOU HAVE A BIG NET?

Hunting for Clues

With recent technology, scientists have developed better tools for predicting how bad storms might be, which helps them send out **evacuation** orders with plenty of time to avoid the storms. High above, satellites and weather balloons gather data on temperature, humidity, and wind speeds. In the water, hurricane **buoys** measure waves and air pressure. Meanwhile, hurricane hunters fly planes loaded with sensors right into growing storms so they can get more accurate information.

In 1943, a flight instructor started hurricane hunting after he bet his students that he could fly into a hurricane safely using special instruments.

Storm hunters must train with the Air Force and the National Ocean and Atmospheric Administration so they can learn how to do their jobs safely.

U.S. hurricane hunters nicknamed two of their planes **Kermit and Miss Piggy!**

One of the newest hurricane tracking tools is a **drone called a Coyote.**

The **Bermuda Triangle** may have earned its reputation as a place where people vanish because strong tropical storms and hurricanes can form there. **Now, technology keeps travelers safe.**

Fighting Hurricanes

As we learn more about each storm, we can figure out ways to stay safer from hurricanes. No one has been able to break up a hurricane or stop one from forming, but scientists keep trying! Meanwhile, the number of hurricane deaths around the world has dropped considerably, despite population growth. Better forecasting and warning systems are saving lives. Property damage is decreasing, too. We've learned how to hurricane-proof buildings and build better levees and seawalls to hold back storm surges.

Scientists tried spraying hurricanes with chemicals that make water freeze. They hoped that would make the storms break apart, but so far it hasn't worked.

If warmth is driving hurricanes, how about pumping cool air into warm oceans? Norwegian scientists plan to try it.

TOO BAD. LET'S TRY THE COLD AIR TREATMENT NEXT!

WELL, I GUESS SPRAYING IT WITH CHEMICALS DIDN'T WORK!

Not all ideas are good. One suggestion was to drop a nuclear bomb into a hurricane! Fortunately, this has not been tried.

Today, people in hurricane-prone areas build sturdier foundations and use stronger materials to help protect buildings.

HOW IS THIS HOUSE STILL STANDING?

IT WAS BUILT TO BE HURRICANE-PROOF!

After Katrina, New Orleans rebuilt and reinforced its levees, canals, water pumps, and seawalls. When Ida came calling in 2021, the new system held!

IT'S THE GREAT WALL OF LOUISIANA TO THE RESCUE!

Your Own Spin

Activity

As a hurricane spins, it travels around a central point. The movement in one part of the spiraling storm is much different than that at another. Which part of a hurricane is the strongest? Find out by making your own mini hurricane!

After a hurricane's eye passes, the wind and rain come back—but from the opposite direction!

What You Will Need

- A large bowl
- Water
- Scissors
- String
- A ruler
- A paper clip
- A large, wooden spoon

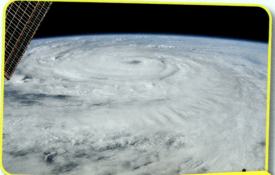

The right side of a hurricane is often the most dangerous when it comes to winds, storm surges, and tornadoes.

Step One

Fill the large bowl two-thirds full of water.

Step Two

Cut a piece of string 10 in. (25 cm) long, and tie one end to the paper clip.

Step Three

Use the wooden spoon to stir the water until it is spinning in a circle.

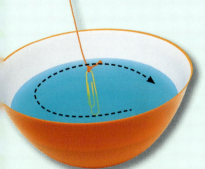

Step Four

While the water is in motion, drop the paper clip into the center of the bowl. Pay attention to how fast the paper clip spins.

Step Five

Stir the water again until it is moving in a circle. This time, drop the paper clip into the bowl along the outer edge of the spinning water. Does the paper clip move more slowly? Does this show that a hurricane is stronger in the center or near its edges?

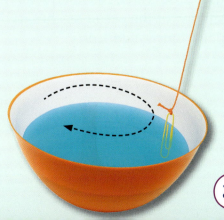

Bermuda Triangle a part of the Atlantic Ocean where ships and planes are said to vanish

buoys floats attached to the bottom of a body of water

climate change the change of Earth's climate and weather patterns, including the warming of Earth's air and oceans, due to human activities

condenses becomes or makes something become more compact

cumulonimbus a thick, tall cloud with fluffy masses at the top

evacuation the removal of people from dangerous places

eye the circular area in the center of a hurricane where the air is calm

eyewall the mass of tall clouds that swirl around the eye of a hurricane

high tide when the natural daily shifting of the ocean reaches its point furthest on land

landfall the arrival of a hurricane to land

levees areas that are built up with earth or other materials to prevent flooding

rainbands curved masses of clouds and wind that are outside the eyewall of a hurricane

Saffir-Simpson Wind Scale a rating system that is used to describe the speed of hurricanes and predict their potential damage

seawalls slopes that are often made of concrete and constructed on shorelines in order to prevent erosion and flooding

spawned gave rise or birth to

wind shear an extreme change in wind speed and direction that takes place over a short distance

Read More

Crane, Cody. *All about Hurricanes (A True Book: Natural Disaster!).* New York: Children's Press, 2021.

Kerry, Isaac. *Climate Change and Extreme Weather (Spotlight on Climate Change).* Minneapolis: Lerner Publications, 2023.

Rossiter, Brienna. *Hurricanes (Severe Weather).* Mendota Heights, MN: North Star Editions, 2023.

Learn More Online

1. Go to **www.factsurfer.com** or scan the QR code below.

2. Enter **"X-treme Hurricanes"** into the search box.

3. Click on the cover of this book to see a list of websites.

Index

alligator alert 21
Bermuda Triangle 25
Bhola cyclone 17
climate change 22
cumulonimbus clouds 11
cyclone 6, 11, 16–17
Cyclone Denise 16
Cyclone Olivia 17
eyewall 10–11
Florida 5
forecasting 14, 26
Great Galveston Hurricane 5
Hurricane Bonnie 11

Hurricane Harvey 21–22
hurricane hunters 24–25
Hurricane Irma 21–22
Hurricane Katrina 15, 20, 27
Hurricane Maria 20, 22
New Orleans, LA 15, 27
storm surge 14–16, 19, 28
technology 24–25
tropical depression 8
tropical storm 8
typhoon 6–7, 16

About the Author

Marcia Abramson is an editor and writer living in southeast Michigan, where they sometimes get leftover rain from hurricanes.